Praise from *The Sender*

Dr. Elko gave me a phrase I used in the 2015 NFC Championship Game: "Live the Moment." I taught that to the team. They did.

Ron Rivera, Head Coach, Carolina Panthers

Dr. Kevin Elko shares a unique lens to view through and a powerful message to grow into. He has a servant's heart that will make you better personally and professionally.

Clint Hurdle, Manager, Pittsburgh Pirates

I have been fortunate to know Dr. Elko, both personally and professionally for over 20 years. I have watched his teaching, insights and creative ideas play a huge role in not only my career, but that of many others in the world of highly competitive sports. He is a tremendous mentor and a great resource for advice. His concepts on training the mind and motivating individuals, are always in the forefront and on the cutting edge!

Butch Davis, Head Football Coach University of Miami,
ESPN Game Day Analyst

Dr. Elko is the best guest in the history of our show. His conversations with us are always compelling and important. His messages to the audience are always heartfelt and filled with compassion. You'll love this book.

Paul Finebaum, Host, *The Finebaum Show*,
SEC Network, ESPN

The message in this book is a game changer that helps people meet their potential. It will transform your life so you can impact others in so many ways. This message has been a part of the culture of our championship teams.

Sarah Patterson, Legendary University of Alabama
Gymnastic Coach

Dr. Elko has been a blessing in my life. I am a better leader and connector because of his guidance. His way of looking at leadership and core values hits home to coaches, men, fathers, and athletes. He is caring and direct and cuts to the point with his own incredible stories and genuine realism. Success as a leader is about connection and Dr. Elko knows exactly how to connect and deliver his message!

Dave Doren, Head Football Coach,
North Carolina State University

Dr. Elko's message on the power of grit had a lot to do with our championship at Florida State—we teach it over and over. The message in this book will take you higher, it did the Noles.

Jimbo Fisher, Head Football Coach,
Florida State University

Dr. Elko's message, which is in *The Sender*, focused our team and was a big part of our run to the College World Series. And it will help elevate your organization to new heights.

Dan McDonnell, Head Baseball Coach,
The University of Louisville

I've known Dr. Elko for almost twenty years. His presence, delivery method, and words are timeless. No matter the audience, he always makes a connection with the audience that makes you feel that he is speaking directly to you. I've personally witnessed him talking to groups ranging from financial advisors to national championship football teams and results are always the same. Everyone leaves his talks with a better understanding of themselves and how life's obstacles are what you make them. He helped me personally in my own fight with cancer and I know that he will help you too.

Tom Moffit, Head Football Strength Coach,
Louisiana State University

This exact message and these letters sent to Coach Pagano are what I listened to as soon as I got my [cancer] diagnosis and started on my journey.

Chris Mortensen, ESPN NFL Analyst

Dr. Elko is the best I've seen in helping young men focus on "keeping the main thing the main thing"! He has given us the tools to help manage daily conflicts and stress while helping our team "lock in" and remove outside distractions. He helps better prepare our student athletes both on and off the field.

Scott Cochran, Head Football Strength Coach,
The University of Alabama

I've known Dr. Elko for a decade. It wasn't until I found myself using his phrases in my everyday life that I realized the profound impact he has had on my life. Through his powerful words and teachings he shows us how to embrace times of challenge with courage, hope, and a little humor.

Greg P. Cicotte, Head of U.S. Wealth Management
and Distribution,
Jackson National Life Insurance Company

the sender

Companion Journal

KEVIN ELKO AND
BILL BEAUSAY

WORTHY®
Inspired

Printed in the United States of America

17 18 19 20 21 22 LBM 10 9 8 7 6 5 4 3 2 1

This book is dedicated to Michael Barnett.
One month before he went to be with the Lord,
Mike gave a talk in Mobile, Alabama. Mike told
the crowd that the message in *The Sender* was a gift
from God. He said that *The Sender* had shown him
to "not waste his cancer." It inspired him to enjoy
each sun rise, treasure his family and to live fully.
He said that it was not a shame that people had to die,
but that so many never lived.
Mike LIVED.

Introduction

When we created *The Sender*, we did so with the simple hope of providing a bright source of encouragement to people fighting for their lives. We hoped a book about a man determined to beat his cancer would be used as inspirational wisdom that people could pass along to loved ones who are in the dark places of health challenges, financial setbacks, family trouble, and more. Now the vision has expanded. We want to focus on you. *The Sender Companion Journal* will encourage you in your walk and help prepare you for your life's difficult tasks. We've included original letters that have never been published and new devotions written to expand the lesson in each letter. As you complete these lessons, you will begin to think and live differently. It had that impact on us. To the best of your ability, pass on what you learn to the next sojourner you cross on the path. God bless you.

This Is Only a Test

Hey, Charlie. Remember those old emergency broadcast system commercial interruptions on TV? The buzzing noise, then the "This has been a test of the emergency broadcast system. Had this been an actual emergency . . ." You remember. Your first instinct was to change the channel to stop the awful noise.

Well, sometimes God conducts those tests on us. He wants to see if you have faith. He wants to see if you'll remain through the test or if you'll change the channel.

Here's a good one: Two men prayed for rain. One just prayed. The other prayed and prepared the fields. Guess which one God was pleased with? He wants to see faith in action. It has to be an intentional, daily commitment to taking action, not changing the channel.

This chemo, your cancer, is a test. He wants to see that you believe in your tools. He wants to see whether you have faith in your treatment. And some people get a test, and they have a testimony. Some people get a test, and they just have a bad case of the moanies. Faith is believing in things you have not seen and the reward you get. With as little moaning as possible.

For the next sixty days, you will be experiencing a test. Don't change channels because this is just a test. A test of your faith in your tools, in your doctors, and in your family. And in Jeremiah 29:11. Remember, God has a plan for you. Don't change the channel.

—The Sender

If *The Sender* is built on a bedrock Scripture, it is Jeremiah 29:11: "For I know the plans I have for you," declares the LORD, "plans to prosper you and not to harm you, plans to give you hope and a future."

The problem is that it's easy to either forget this promise or to live in ways that ignore its power. Can you constantly and willfully focus on this promise? Do you organize your life and your hope around this certainty? Or do you, like many of us, get bogged down and clogged up in our thinking that focuses on the pain and the troubles and not the lesson? Then do you get tired and just flip the channel?

Most of us forget to stay focused on the promise, and it's the cause of a lot of pain. Rather than complain about your pains and troubles, try this: Take a closer look at the pains in your life. Write them down in this journal. Pick the top three. The really bad ones. Then consider the idea that your pain is a pointer. It has a purpose, a message, a power to bring you back to a very real, very big promise: Jeremiah 29:11. Maybe that's what Paul meant when he spoke about being happy for his trials (Romans 5:3–5).

Think on that. See the pointers. Then come back to your life. Live big. No more moanies. Very few people can demonstrate staying on the promise quite like John the Baptist (see Mark 1:6–8). Jesus said there was nobody ever born who was greater than John the Baptist was. Use him as your guide on how to meet your challenges.

_____

_____

_____

_____

_____

_____

_____

---

*John wore clothing made of camel's hair, with a leather belt
around his waist, and he ate locusts and wild honey.
And this was his message: "After me comes the one more
powerful than I, the straps of whose sandals I am not worthy
to stoop down and untie. I baptize you with water,
but he will baptize you with the Holy Spirit."*

MARK 1:6–8

Expect Life to Be Tough/ Align Yourself with Reality

Hey, Charlie. The lesson today is simple: Align your expectations with reality. Someone once said, "Life's really hard." Once you really understand that, the pain of life doesn't matter anymore. You expect it. Because that's what it is. See, I've come to understand that people don't get freaked out because something happens to them; they get freaked out because they thought it would be easier and that bad stuff wouldn't happen to them and they take it personally.

Align yourself with reality; it's not about you.

A team I was once working with was playing for the national championship. The leader of the team stood up and spoke. He didn't yell about how great or tough he was. He didn't thump his chest and brag about how he was going to crush the opponent. No, he was smarter than that. He said simply this: "I expect this game to be the hardest game of my life tomorrow. I expect the guy across from me to be the toughest guy I know. I am going to bring the best me."

Charlie, keep bringing the best you.

What was the difference between those people whom Katrina blew away, including their lives and homes and possessions, and those whom Katrina blew toward a better life? Some are still walking around going, Why? Why did this happen to me? That's the wrong question. The bigger question is always, What am I going to do with it? That's always the bigger question. Align with reality: The storm hit, and it's not about me, so now what am I going to do with it? Align yourself with reality.

Expect life to be tough. And then it doesn't matter anymore. It is what it is. And the question is never, Why? It's always, What am I going to do with it? I love you and I expect it to be tough. But it's not tougher than you.

—*The Sender*

Life is a wonderful gift—a years-long sequence of scenes filled with happiness, hope, disappointment, fulfillment, peace, wrenching pain, and surprises, both good and bad.

It's typically the bad surprises, though, by which we measure the worth of the gift of life we've been given.

That's a really silly measuring stick. As this letter points out, we are all most often crushed by the life surprises that we don't deserve or by times when we feel personally cheated.

But that's not realistic, and that's the point of this letter. Here's the truth: Bad things happen to all of us, all the time. Problems are an integral part of God's plan for you and for me and for everyone, and that is not a bad thing. Stop fighting it or taking it all so personally. When your life is not going so great, it pays to remember that it's part of the plan, and rather than fight it, take a moment to realize it's not personal. It is part of our reality that we need to pursue and understand.

In Psalm 32:8 God says, "I will instruct you and teach you in the way you should go; I will counsel you with my loving eye on you." That's a great comfort if you stop and think about it.

Write down three or four of the pain spots in your life today. Leave room to write between them. Then, go back, and in those blank spaces, write your thoughts and ideas that answer the bigger question: *What am I going to do with this?* If this problem or pain is my Katrina, what is it blowing me toward? Don't be surprised to discover that the more you write and the more you think this way, the more answers will arise. Focusing on this higher vision rewards you with more and better options but only when you change the way you think and align yourself with reality.

For a biblical version of this idea, read Matthew 13:1–23.

As for what was sown on good soil, this is the one
who hears the word and understands it.
He indeed bears fruit and yields, in one case a hundredfold,
in another sixty, and in another thirty.

Matthew 13:23 esv

Have a Game Plan

Charlie. Hope you are well, my man. Here's what your game plan is today: Break free of "me." Your game plan for today is Galatians 6:10. It says to be mindful to do good to others, especially those who are in the family of believers. I want you to purposely live this game plan: to be kind to a number of people today. How? Through encouraging words. A thank-you. A helpful attitude. That's your game plan.

I heard this fella telling a remembrance of his father: "One day my father took the whole family to the circus. And standing there in front of us in line was a family of five. And when this family got up to the window for their tickets and was told the price, the dad's head just dropped. You could tell they didn't have a lot of money, much less the money to get into the circus. His kids were gonna be crushed.

15

"So my father took a twenty-dollar bill out of his wallet and tossed it on the ground. Then he yelled up to the man and said, 'I think you dropped this.' The man turned around and looked at the money being handed to him. He was confused for a second, then he knew. He took the money and bought circus tickets for his whole family.

"Then my dad looked at me and said, 'We are not going to the circus today. I don't have the money for it.'"

That's what he remembered about his dad.

What people will remember about you at the end of this day is your kindness. That's your game plan. And you know me—I've always given you your game plan for the day. That's the one for today.

—*The Sender*

Galatians 6:1–10 is the apostle Paul at his game-planning best: "Carry each other's burdens, and in this way you will fulfill the law of Christ" (vs. 2). Now, of course, Paul directs us to focus this burden carrying on the family of believers, but how about others?

Honestly, we do not like this message much. We are bathed in commercials and subtle media-driven messaging, telling us that the only happy and successful way to live is for "me." We have all been raised to put ourselves in front of everyone else, and we do it very well. We are unconsciously competent and driving ourselves to the front of all lines and ignoring those in our path.

You've heard this before, though, right? None of this talk about self-centeredness is new to us. We've been reminded and warned about our own epic brand of twenty-first-century selfishness. But let's note that the apostle Paul was talking about it too. The reason Paul was even writing about this is because his culture (and the Greek culture of Galatia) was pushing the same "me" thing at the time. And the antidote hasn't changed. It all boils down to making a conscious decision to put others first.

Read Paul's letter carefully. Breaking free of "me" is central to creating a working game plan of your own. It implies that the key to fulfilling the law of Christ is being kind to others and literally forgetting about "me." It's about taking simple action on behalf of others, no matter who they are, what their station in life is, or what they can or cannot do in return for you.

So, stop thinking and start working the game plan. Let go of "me" and serve others. In the end, you get the benefit and the win anyway.

Paul spent a great deal of time in prison. He had lots of time to think and prepare. Take a page out of his game plan. In Acts 16:22–40 we see how Paul planned and prepared. It is a good guideline for us.

Write specific ways you can incorporate Paul's game plan in your life.

About midnight Paul and Silas were praying and singing hymns to God, and the other prisoners were listening to them. Suddenly there was such a violent earthquake that the foundations of the prison were shaken. At once all the prison doors flew open, and everyone's chains came loose.

Acts 16:25–26

Keep the Main Thing
the Main Thing

Hey, Charlie.

Keep the main thing the main thing. Keep your eye on the prize.

In chapter 7 of the book of Judges, Gideon had to go into battle. God told him to take ten thousand men down to the water and ask them to drink. And the ones who put their head all the way down into the water to drink, get rid of them. But the ones who lap the water with their hands but hold their heads up, eyes sharp, keep them. Three hundred soldiers lapped the water with their heads up. And Gideon kept them, and they went on and defeated the Midianites in battle.

There's a place called Shoals Creek. And they have an annual outing for blind golfers. There's this attorney

21

from New Orleans who won eleven years of the seventeen that they did it. And they brought Arnold Palmer in to speak at the evening banquet.

When they met, Palmer said, "That's amazing you golf blind so well."

The guy says, "I'm good. They stand above this hole and they ring this bell and my hearing is so keen from being blind, I shoot the ball to the bell." He went on, "I can beat you."

Palmer chuckled and said, "Wait a minute. I'm Arnold Palmer."

The blind golfer said, "Let's make it interesting. I'll bet you five thousand dollars we go out for eighteen holes, I'll beat you."

Palmer agreed. "When do you want to go out?"

"Tonight at ten o'clock," he replied.

Keep your eyes (and ears) on the prize. Or, as I like to say, "Keep the main thing the main thing."

I want you to just meditate and whisper this to yourself: "I trust my body, I trust my doctors, and I trust God. He has a plan for me that will bring about peace." I want you to just meditate and say this to yourself all the time: Keep the main thing the main thing. Like those men lapping the water, keep your

head up and your eyes on the prize. The prize is peace,
and with peace, your body heals.

—The Sender

God is a ringing bell tinkling in the distance. Have you taught yourself to hear Him?

The third habit in Steven Covey's classic *The 7 Habits of Highly Effective People* is simply this: *Put first things first.* The Sender took it a step further: "Keep the main thing the main thing."

Covey suggested a way to keep the main thing the main thing. He suggested that we order what is important versus what is urgent. He suggested we prioritize our thinking this way:

1. Important and urgent matters
2. Important and not urgent matters
3. Not important and urgent matters
4. Not important and not urgent matters

Philippians 3:7–9 is important and urgent. It's the main thing: "But whatever were gains to me I now consider loss for the sake of Christ."

If you desire to hear the distant and tinkling bell that is

God, you must make faith your main thing. Reading over *The Sender* reminds us that giving up on "me" and all of my accomplishments, and focusing on faith-driven service is the heart of a powerful and transformed life.

Do yourself a favor and write out three things you will do today to stay focused on a life of faith, throwing off your own greatness and listening for the bell. It will tell you where to aim your next shot. And keep repeating the meditation at the end of the Sender's letter: "*I trust my body, I trust my doctors, and I trust God. He has a plan for me that will bring about peace.*"

But whatever were gains to me I now consider loss for the sake of Christ. What is more, I consider everything a loss because of the surpassing worth of knowing Christ Jesus my Lord, for whose sake I have lost all things. I consider them garbage, that I may gain Christ and be found in him, not having a righteousness of my own that comes from the law, but that which is through faith in Christ—the righteousness that comes from God on the basis of faith.

PHILIPPIANS 3:7–9

Put the Marshmallow Down

I'm convinced that cancer is the kind of disease that asks one huge question: How bad do you want it?

A study was done years ago, and I'm probably gonna mess up the details, but they took a group of four-year-olds and accurately predicted their future based on one thing: marshmallows. They put a marshmallow in front of each child with these instructions: "If you eat this one, that's all you get. We'll be back in fifteen minutes. But if you don't eat this one, when we come back in fifteen minutes, you'll get two."

They video-recorded the kids and assigned them to groups: under thirty seconds (before they ate the marshmallow), over thirty seconds, and after fifteen minutes. Then they followed these children for over twenty-five years. The under-thirty-seconds group, well, they didn't do so well. As a group, they ended up generally not going to college, not having that many friends, and having poorer health. The kids who waited over thirty seconds were average on almost all measures. But the "after-fifteen-minutes group" excelled—they had 215 points over average on their college SATs, had better overall health, greater educational attainment, and made more money than the rest of the children did upon reaching adulthood.

How bad do you want it, Charlie? Before you have a testimony, you have to have a test. Don't quit. Gideon went to another general once and said, "My men are fighting weary." And Paul said that if you do not grow weary, you will reap in due season, if you faint not. Fight weary; don't faint, Charlie. And put the marshmallow down.

—The Sender

Before a testimony comes a test. The tests aren't often as easy as saying no to a marshmallow, but the principle is the same. What's the principle?

Wanting something bad in your life goes hand in hand with patience and with what the Sender called "fighting weary." Let's face it. Saying no to the marshmallows in our lives is easy when we're full. It's easy when there is nothing really driving us. But when we are driven, when we are hungry or hurting, saying no to an easy marshmallow is very, very tough.

The Bible teaches us a subtle principle: to be patient in the face of deprivation. Want, pain, and hurt does something beneficial for us. It teaches us, and it molds us in deep and powerful and profound ways that cannot be matched by other means.

Make yourself a "marshmallow list." These are the things that you too easily run to for instant gratification when you might be better off putting them down. It's a discipline to do this, but the Bible is filled with promises to those who endure a difficulty and fight on, while weary.

Do yourself a favor and learn what that means. It's not fun, it's not immediately clear why it's good, and it's not usually what you want. But when you do it anyway see what you learn. Watch yourself grow. And begin the process of seeing a warrior in the mirror.

Read Matthew 4:1–11. These are the marshmallow verses. Jesus Himself wanted the marshmallows, but He demonstrated the correct and powerful way to answer the urge for the immediate in our lives.

---

*The tempter came to [Jesus] and said, "If you are the Son
of God, tell these stones to become bread."
Jesus answered, "It is written: 'Man shall not
live on bread alone, but on every word
that comes from the mouth of God.'"*

MATTHEW 4:3–4

Do You Know
Your 25 Percent?

This man was going into battle, so he went to see the chaplain. He said, "Reverend, we are going into battle tomorrow. I want you to pray for me. I want you to pray that I come out of that battle. I want you to pray that I have favor." The chaplain said, "I can't offer you that prayer. All hell is going to break loose tomorrow, and I can't ask God to have any more favor on you than anyone else here. I just can't offer you that prayer. But I'll go with you. When you go into battle, I'll go right beside you the whole time. I'll go with you."

People sort of have this whole thing about God wrong. I'm sure that there is "favor" with God, though I don't think He has "favorites." What I don't understand is the when or the why of His favor. The timing and selection is just a mystery. But what I am sure about is that God says, "I'll go with you."

Paul prayed to God—and these are my words: "Please change my situation." God replied, "My grace is what I give you. And my grace is sufficient and I will bring you peace beyond understanding. I'll go with you."

Who is going with you, Charlie? I want you to write a list of those people who have gone with you. Make that list. Read it. Just know one thing: I haven't gone through chemotherapy, and I haven't gone through all the fatigue you've gone through. But when you got diagnosed, I got diagnosed with you. You want to know the people on that list. Those are the ones you will keep with you. And that's the list you must read.

I can't ask God to give you favor, but I can go with you.

—*The Sender*

Journals, when used regularly, form a record of your thoughts, reflections, feelings, remembrances, judgments, and logic. Rarely, though, are they used as a tool to sharpen your relationships. And that is one of things they are most useful for.

Here's how you do it. We're reminded of a folksy statistic that may or may not be true, but it still teaches a lesson. The statistic is that 25 percent of your friends really don't like you and never will. Don't be too shocked; we're all in this boat. Another 25 percent don't like you but could be persuaded to like you under the right circumstances. Still another 25 percent like you but could turn cold on you at any moment. And the last 25 percent like you and will like you no matter what. They are your critical 25 percent.

Have you ever read Psalm 139:5–6? Do it now; it's on the next page. What we're saying here is that God has you hemmed in by your critical 25 percent. You're surrounded! That's good news.

Do you know who is who? Do you know who is going with you? Do you know your 25 percent? It's critically important to know. Identify those people and focus your attention on building your relationship and connections with them. Write down their names in this journal. Think about them, pray for them, find articles and stories that would feed their minds and spirits, ask how you can send support back to them. Find out what they need in order to be more effective in their lives and be the person who goes along with them, as well.

Then take a moment and write a list of the people with

whom you will go into battle. It might be family members, old high school friends, new acquaintances, distant relatives, and quite possibly even people you don't quite know yet.

I assure you that, twenty years from now, you'll pick up this book and read these names and be overcome with the realization that both lists are still with you in some way. And it will bring you peace that you took the time to build them up and become necessary to them.

You hem me in, behind and before, and lay your hand upon me. Such knowledge is too wonderful for me; it is high; I cannot attain it.

PSALM 139:5–6 ESV

What Have You Learned?

Charlie, this is a Sunday night letter. There are two kinds of people: those who learn and those who don't. And those who learn, keep on moving up and moving along, and those who don't, keep repeating.

What have I learned? My mother used to always say to me, you either learn or you fail, meaning if you don't learn a lesson, it keeps on trying to teach itself to you.

I didn't want to fail, so I've learned to talk to myself and make sure I understand the lesson. And I sometimes get things very quickly. And sometimes I learn things after a day. But I always say, "I wonder what I've learned? What can I take from this? What can I do differently?"

I am going to ask you a tough question. I want you to sit and pray about it. From what you've gone through these last two weeks, what have you learned? What exactly have you picked up? There are some things I've learned. I used to think that when you get in God's will, life would get easier. But ask the Israelites. When you get in God's will, it gets harder. When they were slaves, nobody was bothering them. But once they were coming out, trying to gain their freedom, and it got harder. You can get crucified in the name of God. Just ask Christ.

What really have you learned? What have you picked up? I love that scene in Rudy *when the priest looks at Rudy and says, "There's two things I've learned from life. One is there is a God, and two, I'm not Him." What have you learned?*

Anne Frank said something like this after her family was taken away during the Holocaust: "In spite of everything, I still believe that people are really good at heart." That's what I've learned. It's powerful. What have you learned? And it's not a bad time on a Sunday night to ask yourself that question.

—The Sender

It seems that life presents us with two big things: lessons to be learned and tasks to be accomplished. And when you miss the lesson or fail the task, it comes around again in the future. Only, when it comes around again, it hurts just a little bit more. In this way, God has provided a mechanism to get our attention and get us to learn and act on what we learn.

Yet the lessons aren't easy to learn unless you are aware that they're persistent and will not go away until you absorb and change. Get ahead of this situation. Take note of the lessons you need to learn by being conscious of the painful areas in your life. We will almost bet that in those areas of pain lie hidden lessons and tasks God wants you to learn or act on.

There is the story in John 8 of Jesus meeting the prostitute who was caught in the act. She's hauled before Jesus and in a highly calculated "gotcha moment" He is asked by the authorities to judge what to do with her. Jesus offers His classic answer ("Let any one of you who is without sin be the first to throw a stone at her") which silences His critics. Then He turns to the woman and offers some more classic wisdom: "Neither do I condemn you. *[Learn your lesson.]* Go now and leave your life of sin" (verse 11, emphasis added).

Write down some lessons you've learned. Then take a yellow highlighter and mark the lessons that you've learned so well that you're not going to repeat them again. Then leave your life of sin.

Everyone in the Scriptures has gone through dark hours of lesson learning. Learn your lessons and be strong.

And David was greatly distressed, for the people
spoke of stoning him, because all the people
were bitter in soul, each for his sons and daughters.
But David strengthened himself in the LORD his God.

1 SAMUEL 30:6 ESV

Full-Crisis Living—
Make Every Day Count

Alright, brother, here we go. Full-crisis living. There was a man named Anthony Burgess. He was diagnosed with a brain tumor. He was given one year to live. But he didn't have one penny to his name. So, he made this plan that he was going to write a novel and make money, so that when he died there would be some money left for his family. He loved it. He got completely involved with writing his novel. It was the most alive and engaged he'd ever felt in his life.

But he didn't die. So, he wrote another novel. And another. He wrote five and a half novels. Still no cancer. He kept writing and eventually wrote seventy novels. He said in one of his books that without the death sentence he'd received, he would have never really lived.

I want you to get fully engaged in something that is not your cancer. Complete living. Full crisis. Having fun.

There are lots of stories like this. The famous writer Norman Cousins got the cancer death sentence and decided to laugh. He watched hours of comedy shows each day. He lived decades longer than his doctors predicted. Another newspaperman named Orville Kelly had what you have. He decided to start a program called MTC: Make Today Count. He lived longer than he was "supposed" to but, more importantly, he lived every day of his life to the fullest.

One of the best aspects of your treatment, Charlie, is to make it your priority to get absorbed in life, to enjoy, to laugh, to smile. That's the biggest aspect of your treatment. God will take care of the rest.

—The Sender

In chapter 12 of the book of Luke, Jesus encourages us to not fret too much about the things of this life, to keep our attention on bigger things (Luke 12:22–32). It's powerful advice that is more powerful when paired with action.

This letter from the Sender is the practical action necessary to put Jesus's advice into play. Being "fully engaged in something that is not your cancer" is how he puts it. Can you get engaged in something that is not your cancer? What is "not your cancer"?

You may or may not have the affliction of cancer, but then again that's not the point here. The point is that cancer reminds the sufferer that it's time to live. Really live. Your problems and trials and tribulations can have the same effect if you let them. They can remind you to start thinking about the things that aren't your troubles and grab ahold of them with appreciation and intention.

In the space below, start making a list of things you are going to get fully engaged with that aren't your problems or your illness. A new hobby? A sport? A recreation or a bucket list item? A family member who you want to get to know better? Let the good things in your life (write them down!) completely attract and absorb you. Make every second count by sticking to this list.

Like us, Christ's followers wanted to know what was next. Jesus didn't tell them, but rather gave them their first lesson in full-crisis living. It's the fabric of a great life. Let your problems drive you to full-crisis living.

_____

_____

_____

_____

_____

_____

_____

_____

_____

_____

_____

_____

*Then they gathered around him and asked him, "Lord,
are you at this time going to restore the kingdom to Israel?"
He said to them: "It is not for you to know the times
or dates the Father has set by his own authority.
But you will receive power when the Holy Spirit
comes on you; and you will be my witnesses in Jerusalem,
and in all Judea and Samaria, and to the ends of the earth."*

ACTS 1:6–8

09

Me and the Pope:
Cut Out What's
Not Necessary

Alright, Charlie. Believe it or not, I got a phone call yesterday from the office of the Holy Father. I asked, "Who's the Holy Father?" They tell me it's the pope and he's going to use one of my newsletters in a homily. I kid you not. I said, "What's a homily?" So, here goes with the pope's homily.

I went to New York shortly after 9/11, and they introduced me to a security guard who was in Building One at the World Trade Center. When the planes hit, he was in the stairwell yelling at the women to take off their heels so they could descend the stairs faster. He started to cry—he said people died because they wouldn't take their heels off.

What do you want? Peace? Joy? Health? Take your heels off. Get rid of everything that is not peace, joy, and health, and better health will find you. For example, if you want peace, let go of your need to be right and peace will find you. Take your heels off. Let it go.

Now, let me show you what made it to the Vatican. Ready? "You don't need to find God. Get rid of everything in your life that isn't God, and God will find you." God wants to know right now that the only thing that you want in your life is to completely restore your body so you can restore Him, and you can restore Him in the hearts of people. Not my will but Thy will be done, O Lord.

—The Sender

(This is kind of a crazy story, but like all the other letters in *The Sender*, it's true. We don't know that the pope quoted Kevin by name, but the story is true.)

Here's the heart of this particular letter, and in some ways the heart of the whole message of *The Sender*: "You don't need to find God. Get rid of everything in your life that isn't God, and God will find you."

How do you do that?

Ecclesiastes 3:1–13 is one of our favorite passages for

this because in many respects it points the way to getting rid of things in our lives that aren't God so that He may find us. Find these verses in your Bible and read them carefully. Then, write down in the space on the following pages the specific "times" that are showing up in your life right now. Is it time to grieve or time to share? Is it time to complain or time to encourage others? Is it time to be depressed or time to look for opportunities to serve others? Is it time to make war or time to make peace? What time is it in your life right now?

Here's a head start: It's time to concentrate on the things that your problems and disabilities don't prevent you from doing. It's time to stop regretting what you can't do and focus on what you can do. It's time to enable your spirit rather than focus on the things that dispirit you. It's time to tell others about your blessings rather than share your curses.

Do those things, and God will show up in ways you can't imagine.

Keep showing up in this way, and maybe your words will even cross the lips of the pope!

_____

_____

_____

_____

_____

_____

_____

_____

_____

_____

_____

_____

_____

_____

_____

_____

_____

_____

There is a time for everything, and a season
for every activity under the heavens.

ECCLESIASTES 3:1

10

Constant Prayer

Charlie, the Scriptures say that we should be in constant and continuous prayer. I read that and thought to myself, Don't you have to work? Don't you have to walk around? Don't you have to do other things? Do you just sit next to the bed all day on your knees with your eyes closed? How do you do that?

My sister was in pre-med, and she came home one day and she saw me at thirteen years old looking in the mirror. She said, "What's wrong with you?" I said, "I don't want to go bald." And she said, "I learned in school that if you tend to think about something a lot, it will happen. The way I understood that is if you sit around thinking about going bald, you'll lose all your hair."

Yikes, Dog!

Worry is praying for what you don't want. Remember this lesson from Job 3:25 (ESV): "The thing that I fear comes upon me, and what I dread befalls me." What do you worry about? Stop accidentally praying for what you don't want. You create your world. What do you want, Charlie? A healthy body? Hair? Spend time thinking about a healthy body and other good things.

I'm going to view myself as healthy constantly. And I'm gonna think about a lot of thick hair.

—The Sender

This is a crazy idea, isn't it? That "worry is praying for what you don't want"? We often think that if we spent half the time we spend worrying on something more productive, it's no telling what might happen.

This isn't just a crazy idea. Help yourself to the wisdom here: Think about some of the things you will worry about, regret, loathe, and have anxiety about today. Crazy! You know already what you're going to fret about! Somewhere deep in your mind you've got a "to do" list of things to pray about! Now write in the lines below a positive aspect of each that you can pray for. Pray for what you want!

Don't think you're alone. We are all like this. We've all become accidental experts in the arena of worry.

Go look in the mirror and see a new image. See a person who is born in the image of God. See someone for whom God has created a great and wonderful plan. See the person who God sees, not the person your burdens force in front of you.

First Corinthians 13:12 talks about this process directly. Only we're not using it as a metaphor: When we look in the mirror understand that we only see one version of ourselves looking back. God wants a new vision to come into focus. He wants us to think about a new vision with the same constancy that we usually give our worries.

Now, today, as you find yourself going deep into accidental prayer about your worry, quickly think back to the mirror. See the new person there, and thank God for new chances, new visions, and new prayers.

_____

_____

_____

_____

_____

_____

_____

_____

_____

_____

_____

_____

_____

_____

_____

_____

_____

*Therefore, if anyone is in Christ, the new creation has come:
The old has gone, the new is here!*

2 CORINTHIANS 5:17

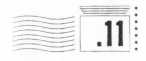

Attitude

Greetings, Charlie. What we are doing here with these letters is like the apostle Paul's ministry. His ministry included writing letters to churches like Corinth and Ephesus. Letters. There's a saint, Saint Teresa of Lisieux. She died real young. Her whole ministry was nothing more than letters to her sister. And the purpose was attitude. To be mindful of attitude.

I don't think anything is more important to beat cancer than attitude. So here is a key point: Attitude is not a gene; it's a muscle. You told me last week that your attitude had slipped a little bit. It slips because we need a daily workout. If you don't exercise a muscle, it atrophies. If you don't exercise your attitude, it atrophies.

So I want you to have a workout that you do twice a day, a meditation before you go to bed as you are going to sleep, just whispering to yourself, "God has a plan for me, Jeremiah 29:11," and again in the morning. Just let it roll off your tongue.

Meditate on it over and over. God has a big plan for me. And everything that is happening is in His plan. And you just go to bed with that on your mind. It is very important what we go to bed with. And you let your body heal all night long with the thought, God has a big plan for me.

—The Sender

Jesus spent a lot of time alone. Scripture indicates that He often retreated by Himself in the morning time. We can only assume that He was spending time in the presence of God through prayer and meditation. He took care to build up His attitude muscles on purpose.

The workout schedule the Sender gives to Charlie is twice a day. That might sound like a lot, but when you start doing it, you'll be very surprised to find out how easy it is to take just a few minutes out of your schedule, twice a day, in order to disconnect, refresh, and reboot.

I am going to ask you do something you might think is crazy. I want you to write down a reminder in this journal that you'll take fifteen minutes twice a day and just be alone and quiet with yourself. No phones, no social media, no kids, no connection to the outer world (as much as is possible). If you're a single mother or father, it might be in those moments before your kids awaken and after your kids fall asleep. If you're a busy person working three jobs, it might be in those moments when you're driving and you have just a very short amount of time to call your own. You might be one of those people who is constantly surrounded by chaos and action all the time. But take the time. Seize the time to reorient your attitude.

Winston Churchill once said that there is never a good time for a vacation, so just take one anyway. Nobody is going to just give you the time needed to do this, so you must take it for yourself. It's an attitude workout that makes you stronger and better.

It might be the best part of your day. And you WILL NOT REGRET IT!

------

*Yet the news about him spread all the more,
so that crowds of people came to hear him
and to be healed of their sicknesses.
But Jesus often withdrew to lonely places and prayed.*
LUKE 5:15–16

One-Way Missionaries: Go Be Necessary

Hi, Charlie. About two hundred years ago, there was something called a "one-way missionary." A one-way missionary buys a coffin, puts all of his clothes in it, then buys a one-way ticket to wherever he's going. A. W. Milne was a Scottish missionary to Africa, working with the Pygmies. Other missionaries went before him, and they were all killed. But he said that in order to do God's work, he needed to be fully committed. To be fully necessary.

Edward Everett Hale summed up that idea with his quote, "I am only one, but still I am one. I cannot do everything, but still I can do something; and because I cannot do everything, I will not refuse to do something that I can do." And I would add, that which I must do, standing in God's grace, I will do.

To your Maker you are necessary. So, let's get completely well so He will reveal to us the next step in our being necessary to Him. Be necessary, Charlie. And you don't know the next step of His plan, so quit thinking about it. Don't think, The next step is this or that. No. He will tell you. Just be necessary.

I don't know what the plan is. And you are making a mistake if you sit and wonder what it is. God reveals the plan to us as we go. He never lets us know what it is. He just says to get ready, because He has something around the corner and He needs you.

—The Sender

This is a fascinating, true historical anecdote. And the finish to the story of A. W. Milne will inspire you. It started around the turn of the nineteenth century, when a group of Scottish churchmen became known as "one-way missionaries." They gained this name because they gathered up all of their belongings, put them into a coffin, and bought one-way tickets to all parts of the globe. They knew they'd never come home again.

A. W. Milne was one such man. He felt called to minister to a group of Indonesian headhunters who had martyred every other person who tried to do mission work there. He was accepted and lived for thirty-five years with them, translating their language and building a life with them. He never returned to Scotland.

When he died, his beloved tribe buried him in the village and wrote the following words on his tombstone: "When he came there was no light. When he left there was no darkness."

Milne understood what it meant to "go be necessary."

If you want to understand what the Bible means about being necessary, read Luke 10. Read all of it. Earlier in this chapter, Jesus was choosing and preparing His team to go before Him as He headed to Jerusalem for Passover for what would be His crucifixion and resurrection. As you will read, He is very serious in the early part of this chapter about getting his team right.

But then He tells them what is probably one of the most profound pieces of godly wisdom He could bestow on them as they left. He gives them the parable about the good Samaritan. In this story, Jesus taught them that the biggest part of the question of eternal life and doing God's will is taking care of your neighbors. Being necessary. And the disciples spent the rest of their lives doing just that.

Keep moving. Keeping being necessary, and then let God show up.

Write specific ways you can keep moving and being necessary, and then let God show up.

_You shall love the Lord your God with all your heart
and with all your soul and with all your strength
and with all your mind, and your neighbor as yourself._

LUKE 10:27 ESV

You Can't Share Preparation

Charlie . . . got a funny story for you. This mean old woman goes into a store complaining, "every time I come into this store, you don't have the book I want. I'm so tired of it!" The young man behind the counter said, "What's the book you want, ma'am?" She said, "I want a book called How to Remain Young and Beautiful.*" The guy behind the counter said, "I will order that book for you right now and I will mark it URGENT!"*

Pretty funny. Here's a lesson: There is no urgent. There is only prepared and not prepared. And you can't share your preparation.

I remember the first time I heard the story of the ten wise and the ten foolish bridesmaids in the Scriptures. In my own words, what happened was that the wise bridesmaids got oil and trimmed their lamps, so that when the groom came they could see him. And the foolish ones didn't. And then, when the bridegroom came, the foolish ones asked the smart ones for some oil. But they said no. That didn't sound very "Christian" to me. But then I realized what it meant: The oil represented preparation. And you can't share preparation. One ballplayer who prepares for the game cannot just give his preparation to a ballplayer who didn't prepare.

Attitude requires preparation. Preparing daily. You build it; you don't borrow it.

—The Sender

We'd like to offer some encouragement here that's a little different from the other entries in this journal. The very fact that you are here, reading and filling these pages, says something quite profound about you: You are a preparer. Research has shown that nearly 80 percent of people look outside of themselves for the source of their troubles and the answers. But you look inside. By writing, thinking, journaling, and preparing, that's what you're doing. That's no small thing.

Writing and interacting with this journal is an act of bringing oil for your lamp. Take a moment and tell yourself "congratulations." Really . . . as people of faith, it's way too common to look at our own defects and weaknesses and judge ourselves with some negativity, never appropriately crediting ourselves for the good we've done. Don't do that to yourself. Give credit where credit is due.

We've long believed that if you don't carefully and realistically consider the conflicts and cares you carry around in your head, they will get the best of you. If your troubles control you (and only you know whether or not they do), they control that battle space that is your life. If things often become urgent in your life, it's because the cares and worries of your life have taken the place of daily preparation for the battle.

There is only prepared and not prepared in the fight of life. Doing this journal with consistency and realism and care *is* preparing. Congratulations. And remember that preparation is a daily pursuit. Without it, life's situations can go from manageable to suddenly urgent in no time flat. List the cares and worries that are trying to take control of your life. Prepare today and get ready to finish better. Get your oil, trim your lamp, look at your battle space, and prepare.

*Prepare your work outside; get everything ready for yourself
in the field, and after that build your house.*

PROVERBS 24:27 ESV

Believe Well

Hi, Charlie. Here's your lesson in this letter: Get ready to fight. When King David was getting ready to fight Goliath, he went to King Saul and said, basically, "I can beat that giant. I'm going to beat that giant."

Here's the point. Ready? You aren't going to beat this because you fight well. David beat Goliath because he believed well.

I want to talk about David and the way he believed. There's a man named Benaiah. Have you ever heard of Benaiah? No one has ever heard of Benaiah. When David became king, Benaiah was chosen to be his chief of bodyguards. Sort of like the head of the Secret Service. What did Benaiah ever do to deserve this honor? From the biblical account, I imagine it went something like this: One day a lion came into his village and he faced the lion. He sprinted at the lion, not away from the lion. Most people run away from the lions in their marriage, the lions in their health, the lions on their team, the lions in their company. But not Benaiah. He ran right at it.

The lion then turned and ran and fell down into a snowy pit. Benaiah jumped down into the pit and killed the lion with his hands. Benaiah did not kill the lion because he fought well. He wasn't bold because he fought well. It was because he believed well. That's what people miss. Believing well.

People who believe big ask big. I want you to start asking bigger. I want you to ask bigger of the doctors. Ask bigger of your treatment. Start asking. Start getting bold. Believe even more. Alright, my man. Go get 'em. Even bigger. Up a notch.

—The Sender

"Run toward the sound of the guns" is an old military refrain that we'd do well to build into our own belief practices. It's something that Benaiah knew well, and it won him acclaim. It's hard to describe the power that comes over a person who, rather than run in fear at life's problems, turns, faces the trouble, and attacks. It's the basic element of "believing well."

Believing well is a decision. It's often a messy, difficult, scary, and tense moment when people decide to believe well and take a leap of faith. But something always happens when someone takes that leap. They're often overcome by a sense of calm, of purpose, of certainty. Yes, you can literally create a sense of peace, purpose, and focus right now while facing your big troubles head-on and attacking in faith.

We know that is easy to say, but how do you get started? The lines that follow below this entry are blank. Sort of like the next twenty-four hours of your life. Yes, you have things you need to get done and areas that will demand your focus, but in reality, how you are going to react is unscripted. Unless you do one thing right now: Make a decision to go higher, to live bolder, more peaceful, and more faithful.

Decide that now. Don't decide to transform your whole life—just the next twenty-four hours. If that is too much, then just commit to changing the next hour, or the next fifteen minutes, or the next minute. The time frame does not matter. What matters is taking conscious control; believe big, asking God big and then taking action. Psalm 138:3 says, "When I called, you answered me; you greatly emboldened me."

Up a notch, Dog. Attack time. That's all.

_____

_____

_____

_____

_____

_____

_____

_____

_____

_____

_____

_____

_____

_____

_____

_____

_____

_____

_____

Fight the good fight of the faith. Take hold of the eternal life to which you were called when you made your good confession in the presence of many witnesses.

1 TIMOTHY 6:12

When It Rains, I'm Gonna Let It

Hi, Charlie. It's raining today, and it reminds me of a story. There was a man who took his wife on a second honeymoon in the Smokey Mountains. It rained the whole time. As they were getting ready to leave the rustic old mountain lodge where they had stayed, they passed this old guy on his front porch with his feet up on an old barrel and a pipe in his mouth. The old guy was just smiling. Intrigued, the husband looked at the old man and said, "How can you just sit there while it rains and smile?" The old man took the pipe out of his mouth and said, "Son, I decided a looooong time ago that if it decides to rain, I'm gonna let it."

I so wish you weren't going through this struggle. But I've thought about it and I've prayed about it. Be where your feet are. Take this completely in trust that the life you go back to will be incredible. Just let it be and let it go.

—*The Sender*

This short anecdote bristles with timeless wisdom. But it's hard wisdom: The absolute toughest thing in the world for us to do is to "let go and let God." Why is this so hard?

It's probably because we've learned to fight, or we've been taught or conditioned to fight out our lives like we're Butch Cassidy and the Sundance Kid. The New Testament teaches us a radically different approach to the conflicts and trouble that silhouette normal life. Jesus teaches us a subtler and vastly more difficult way of handling our ongoing struggles with the world.

That's right. Being a peacemaker, a lover of people, and a source of good is difficult most of the time, if not, at the very least, inconvenient. Fighting it out might just come easier to us because it's what we've always known. But we're being called to a different approach, and even if we're strongly ambivalent about adopting it, it is a better way.

How do you do it?

We call Ephesians 4:31–32 the "deep let-go" passage. Read it. What is Paul telling us? He's saying that bitterness, anger, rage, fighting, and slander are the source of major distractions and ongoing pain. But then he offers the ultimate solution: Be kind, compassionate, and forgiving. To everyone. At all times. For no particular reason. For no real justification. For no cost. For no quid pro quo. Just do it.

Wow! When you let go of those things for no reason other than to have a forgiving and compassionate heart about you, you gain access to a great and wonderful, sweeping and refreshing "let go."

Forgive people as you've been forgiven. Who will you forgive? Love people as you've been loved. Who will you love? Be kind and compassionate as a way of thinking and living. And enjoy a refreshing shower of relief.

There is a nice breeze today.

_Let all bitterness and wrath and anger and clamor
and slander be put away from you, along with all malice.
Be kind to one another, tenderhearted,
forgiving one another, as God in Christ forgave you._

Ephesians 4:31–32 esv

To Where Will You Shift?

Charlie. I read a book by a famous cancer psychologist once that said the moment a person learns they have cancer, there's a shift in their psyche. Almost within seconds, something very important happens. Things that seemed so important prior to the diagnosis are suddenly dismissed. In an instant. And then there's a new importance. And it's not working for the weekend or the next big deal or buying a new house.

I wonder where you are going to shift? Maybe it's suddenly more important to go see your kids or your parents. Maybe it isn't so important to have that last word in a fight with your spouse. Maybe the dandelions in your yard don't matter so much anymore. It's interesting, isn't it?

A man who lives five doors from me was diagnosed with the exact same cancer Steve Jobs was diagnosed with. Almost on the same day. He outlived Steve Jobs by about a year, believe it or not. He wasn't supposed to. But he wrote a letter to all his friends at Christmastime, describing how he was going to finish his life.

If you wrote a letter like that today, what exactly would you write? What would it say? I keep this card in my wallet; it was given to me by Paul Bear Bryant's son, because Paul Bear Bryant kept this in his wallet:

"This is the beginning of a new day. God has given me this day to use as I will. I can waste it or use it for good. What I do today is very important, because I'm exchanging a day of my life for it. When tomorrow comes, this day will be gone forever, leaving something in its place I've traded for it. I want this to be a gain, not a loss. Good, not evil. Success, not failure. So, I don't forget the price I paid for it."

—*The Sender*

If you are of a certain age, you will remember the original movie *The Planet of the Apes*. The most shocking and memorable scene is the very last one. Charlton Heston is on what we believe is some planet in the future where apes rule. After a time of brutal enslavement and cruelty, he, a human, is able to escape his primate tormenters.

As he trots on a horse down a beach, he comes across a sight that changes everything: The Statue of Liberty is sticking up out of the sand! In one instant, the whole meaning and message of the movie shifts. He's not on a distant planet; he's been on Earth the whole time. We humans blew it somehow, and the whole world is now run by monkeys.

In some less-than-profound way, this is the story of anyone who undergoes a profound event in their life. Suddenly what you thought was totally true and real and important, has been radically shifted.

Consider Paul's journey to Damascus in Acts 9. Nobody had more reason to be completely impressed with their own accomplishments and station in life than Paul (see Philippians 3:4–8). But when that bright light came on that nice day with the voice and the call to do something new, Paul knew his life had changed. He could tell you all about this kind of instant mind-shift.

To what will you shift? In the space provided after this message, write your "finishing letter," like the man in *The Sender* did. How are you going to finish your life? To what are you going to shift? Then, taking a tip from the great coach "Bear" Bryant himself, copy the letter and carry it with you from now on. Literally take a pair of scissors and cut out a version of your letter that will fit into your purse or wallet. If what you shift to is important enough to write in your journal, let it be important enough to be the new standard by which you live your life and carry with you constantly. Be serious about this, and the payoff might be a hall-of-fame type of life.

[Saul] fell to the ground and heard a voice say to him,
"Saul, Saul, why do you persecute me?"
"Who are you, Lord?" Saul asked.
"I am Jesus, whom you are persecuting," he replied.
"Now get up and go into the city,
and you will be told what you must do."
ACTS 9:4–6

Finding God in Walmart

Charlie, it's me. I love Job 42:5. It says, and I'm para-phrasing, "I have heard about you with my ears. But now I have seen you with my spiritual eyes." It's ironic, but this comes at the end of the story, after everything Job had been through. He says, "Before I only heard of you; now I've seen you. "

You won't believe this, but on every Christmas Eve our family goes out to find God. Do you know where we find Him? Walmart.

I stuff money in my kids' pockets at Walmart. And then we wait, and my kids just walk around the cash registers. You know, at Christmas Eve some mother looks at the presents their kids will get the next morn-ing, and they don't have much—a single parent, for instance. At the last minute, they are always trying to buy a bicycle or something more. You would be shocked at how many bicycles come through Walmart on Christmas Eve. And you can look, and you can just see that that poor mother has next to nothing to pay for the extra toys.

So, my kids walk up at the last minute and pay for the bikes with cash. And the mothers always grab my kids and hug them. And I don't always find God in church on Christmas Eve, but I always find Him in Walmart.

Charlie, list all the times you've seen God. And just start saying, "God, I see You." There's a Scripture that says that no one has ever seen God. But when one person loves another, God is there. Job said, "I have heard of You with my ears. But I've finally seen You with my eyes."

—*The Sender*

Do you ever hear yourself say something to the effect of, "God, where are You?" It might come at the strangest of times: times of peak adversity and trouble, times of pressure and difficulty and more. It just seems that seeking God's whereabouts during tumult is all too common.

What you might find most interesting, though, is that the Scriptures talk a lot about seeing God but not solely during times of trouble. Check out Jeremiah 29:13 or

Proverbs 8:17 for just two examples of seeking God even when things are going just fine. That theme is all over the Scriptures.

Yet way too often, the only time we seem genuinely serious about actually finding God is when life's troubles hit us hard.

This is a habit that has a remedy. Though the story of Walmart and the kids is very true, you needn't wait till Christmas Eve or aim yourself directly at the people around you. Go seek His people and you will see God. People and hearts and needs are ever present. The places we can find God are all around us, as are the rich opportunities to serve those who are badly in need. Want to find God? Look around just about anywhere.

If you change your focus and sharpen your eyes in this way, you will have many places at which you can say "God, I see You." In fact, begin the lifestyle of serving others now, and you'll find the journal pages following to be way too few to record all the God sightings you'll soon encounter.

Try it and see.

Let each of us please his neighbor for his good,
to build him up.

ROMANS 15:2 ESV

Misery into Ministry

Alright, Charlie, it's me. I might have mentioned this idea before, but it's so good. I'm speaking to Pitt, the University of Pittsburgh football team, and they are getting ready for their upcoming season. My little boy was there, and my wife and my little girl were too. They sat in the back. My little boy was four years old, and I made this statement to the entire team: "Worry is praying for what you don't want." I got that from Job 3:25, which says, "What I feared has come upon me; what I dreaded has happened to me."

So, we go home that night and lightning starts to hit, and in the middle of the night, my little girl, Claire, wakes us all up about two in the morning crying. We all go into her room. We're trying to calm her down, and my little boy says, "I want to speak."

"Wait a minute, Jared. We are trying to calm down Claire."

"I want to speak," he insists.

"Go ahead," I said finally.

"Claire, didn't you hear what Daddy said today? You are in here praying for what you don't want." We all about fainted.

So, here's what I want you to do, Charlie. I want you to keep on chanting, "God has a plan for me." I want you to keep visualizing dancing at your daughter's wedding. I want you to visualize handing me a state championship ring after you win it.

I want you to keep on visualizing and saying to yourself, "I am going to change lives with what I've got. I want to take my misery and make it my ministry." Whatever is true, whatever is honest, whatever is pure. Whatever is lovely. Think about those things. And when you start off the day, just write a little note and put it in your pocket and let that come off your tongue all day long.

—*The Sender*

Have you ever felt as though you just had nothing to offer anyone? Maybe you'd just been so beat up, so mired down, so sick and exhausted that you just had nothing left?

Maybe, even worse, you felt that as a result of your trouble, you had no standing or credibility to even open your mouth about anything?

Turning your mistakes or bad breaks into a source of super-strength is not a common way to think. But it is a biblical way to think.

If you take the time to really grasp the story of *The Sender*, you will realize that it is a tale of active, conscious, and intentional redemption. It's about taking your life troubles and squeezing out of them wisdom and depth. It's about letting the events of your life shape you and prepare you on purpose. We love those kind and wise words of Helen Keller, who said, "Face your deficiencies and acknowledge them; but do not let them master you. Let them teach you patience, sweetness, insight."

The Sender couldn't have put it better. Don't deny or downplay the very lessons God put in your way to make you better. Rather, use them as a catapult to launch you into a life that serves others because of what you have gone through and learned.

On the lines below, write down the worst thing you've ever done, or the worst calamity or illness you've endured. It does not matter whether the problem was one of your own making or whether you were victimized by an illness or a life compromise. Just write it down. Then, next to it, write out three ways in which that experience could be actively built into a lesson that you could use to help someone else. This is a very practical way to take a lesson that hurt you and turn it into a ministry. Your ministry.

_____

_____

_____

_____

_____

_____

_____

_____

_____

_____

_____

_____

_____

_____

You have turned for me my mourning into dancing;
you have loosed my sackcloth and clothed me with gladness.
PSALM 30:11 ESV

.19

What's the Chemo Killing, Charlie?

Charlie, what exactly is this struggle, this chemo treatment, actually killing? Moses was a Hebrew boy, raised as an Egyptian. He liked Hebrew food and Hebrew culture, but he lived in an Egyptian palace. I think he had kind of an inner fight, an identity crisis going on inside of him. Was he Egyptian or Hebrew? There he was, an Egyptian army officer, a member of the Egyptian royal family, and yet also a Hebrew slave. And one day he's looking out and he sees an Egyptian soldier fighting with a Hebrew slave, and he kind of found out who he was. He jumped in and killed the Egyptian.

It's funny in a way what comes out when we struggle. Slowly but surely, what you are not gets killed off.

Martin Luther King Jr. said that some of us are

Cadillacs and some of us are Fords. And once we admit to ourselves that we are a Ford, we can get into parking places that a Cadillac could never get into.

The bad parts of your struggle are easy to see, like pain, nausea, dry mouth, exhaustion. But, Charlie, I've watched you and I know you—and who you are not has died. Who you are—a loving man, a leader, someone whom others care about, someone who inspires other—that part lives on.

So, every time you go through this struggle, remember that the chemo isn't just killing the cancer; it's killing something else. It's letting the Hebrew slave come out. Alright, my man. Just let it kill away what you are not.

—The Sender

Here's a thought that may have never crossed your mind before: The trials and illnesses that you're experiencing not only make you suffer, but conversely, they provide the opportunity to kill off what is not you. We tend to think that if we can just hurry up and survive the next onslaught of trouble, we can get back to who we were/are and life as we knew it. Quickly. But what if you began thinking differently? What if you began thinking that this trial or illness is the path to a totally new way of living? A little longer and not so fun a path, but a necessary one to take you to the next level?

It's hard to change to this way of thinking, because we are so used to fleeing pain. We define it as "bad" and something to be avoided at all costs. But that is not how God sees pain at all. God sees pain in a more purifying and productive sense. Not in the sense that He's a sadist who draws pleasure from watching us squirm, but as a loving Father who knows that He must first get our attention, and then induce a change.

If nothing else, the Bible is about transformation. The old is gone and the new is come (see 2 Corinthians 5:17). You've got a new mind (see Romans 12:2); a new heart (see Ezekiel 36:26); a new life (see John 3:3). And that's not even mentioning being born again! Personal transformation is a cornerstone of our faith. And our pain can be used as motivation to take us right to it.

Rather than curse God for your pains, learn to leverage those pains to help knock off the crusty outer shell of who you think you are, and be transformed into the deeper being whom God has built you to be. That's moving to the next level. No going back.

Always be thinking, *What is this trial killing in me?* Take time to ponder this question and write about your transformations.

*Since we have these promises, beloved, let us cleanse
ourselves from every defilement of body and spirit,
bringing holiness to completion in the fear of God.*

2 Corinthians 7:1 esv

20

Get Simple

Charlie, it's me. You know one thing that I've learned in football, but that I honestly think escapes most coaches, is that complex problems require simple thinking. Like when your situation gets a little complicated, you need to get a little bit more simple.

There once was a famous rabbi named Chafetz Chaim, from Poland. An American tourist was coming through Poland and wanted to visit him. And Rabbi Chafetz Chaim had hardly any possessions, hardly anything at all. The American tourist said, "Where in the world are your possessions?" The rabbi said to the tourist, "Where are yours?" The tourist, not having much with him, said, "But I'm just passing through." The rabbi said, "So am I."

There was once another man who had a seven-way heart bypass. And after he got done with his surgery, three days later, they took him out to walk for twenty-five steps. Then the next day, twenty-five more steps. Until he got up to four times a day going up and down the hallway. One day when he was walking up the hall, he looked into a room and there were two heart patients sitting there with their IVs, just lying back. And he said to the nurse, "My goodness, those people have it so much worse than I do." She said, "No, they don't. They just see themselves as heart attack victims and they gave up. You are trying to get better."

I don't want you to ever see yourself as a cancer victim. I want you to keep on thinking real simple, like this: I'm just trying to get better. Real simple. I don't think I'm snake bit. I don't think anything's wrong. I've got a real simple head. I'm just getting better.

When complex things happen, we usually want to think up complicated answers. But the answer is to get simple.

—The Sender

Not long ago four-star Admiral William "Bill" McCraven, the head of the United States Special Operations Command (Special Forces), gave the commencement address at his alma mater, the University of Texas. In this memorable talk (available on youtube.com), he talks about taking the simple approach to changing the world from the perspective of Navy Seal training. He told the crowd that the first lesson he learned as a Navy Seal was that if you want to change the world, you must start by making your bed.

Jesus often spoke of approaching life with this Navy Seal focus on simplicity. He knew that life can become a mental tornado, and the worst thing you can do is intentionally (or accidentally) complicate it. Listen to almost everything He says: When people wanted to follow Him, He spoke of leaving everything behind. When He sent His followers out, He told them to take very little with them. The message He taught His disciples to preach was a simple message that pointed people to God. He talked about love, service, compassion, and giving. He talked about healing the sick and being with the downtrodden. Simple, simple, simple.

Rare is the person who can stay focused on a simple idea for very long. Our pace and style of life does not encourage this. But it never has. Life has presented complications to every human being who has truly tried to live it. Address the complications in your own life. In the space below, write out some very simple words that define who you are and who you want to be today. Just one or two words. Nothing complex, nothing over the top. Don't allow your life to become a Ph.D. dissertation. Your life and tasks and lessons are a road that needs to be traveled, and like Jesus has said, the lighter the better.

Not long ago I heard someone say this succinctly and with power: "Appreciate everything. Want nothing. Have everything." Good advice. Take your word or two below and make them your focus today. If you can't manage it for the whole day, try it for an hour. Just let those words hover in your mind. Feel the power of simplicity.

Did you make your bed this morning? If not, go back and start your simplified life there.

For my yoke is easy and my burden is light.

MATTHEW 11:30

21

I'm Working

Late one day a visitor came to see Michelangelo in his studio. The great artist was just sitting in the middle of his studio staring at this tall square block of marble. His assistant told the visitor he'd been there all day, just staring at that block of marble. So, the visitor approached the great man and asked, "What are you doing?" Michelangelo broke his gaze and, turning to the visitor, said simply, "I'm working."

The marble he was staring at would become his masterpiece, King David. But even the great master knew he could not take the first chip off of that block until he could see what it would be in the end. Then his task was clear: All he had to do was chip away what was not King David.

Do you have a very specific model with your health? I told you the other day that my mother was diagnosed with lung cancer and was down to not much time. Just over a week, as it turned out. And I got together with my sisters and asked them to think about how we wanted the last part of her life to go. And I asked them specifically what we wanted our role to be in that. We had to decide fast and we had to be specific. Then when we were clear, we could get to work. But not until we had that vision. Just keep on thinking and meditating and praying: What do I want? Let's keep chipping away what's not it. Alright, my man.

—*The Sender*

A study conducted by *USA Today* questioned people about what prompted them to get up in the morning. It was expected that they might get reactions like, "I've got a great life," or "I have to get the kids going," or "It's great to be alive." That's not exactly what they found. According to the study, eight out of ten people got up in the morning because they had to use the bathroom.

Imagine, with this glorious gift of life awaiting, people have to be pried out of bed with the crowbar of a full bladder!

A lot of people—a *lot*—have no compelling vision for their own lives. Not only do they not have a compelling vision, but they actually have no vision at all. And you can't get the vision from a guru or read it or buy it online. And nobody else can see it for you. It needs to come from your heart as God reveals it. And you have to listen carefully, and it's not easy to do. It's no wonder, really, that so many people lead such dispassionate, plodding, and routine lives. Nothing burns inside of them. They just haven't patiently taken up the task of looking at themselves till they see it.

You probably aren't a sculptor like Michelangelo, but you *are* the sculptor of your own life. I want to challenge you with a simple idea: The blank lines following represent a block of white marble. They can be whatever you want them to be. On them, you can create a map for your own *King David* of a life, or you can leave it blank. It's your life and your life alone. It's a gaping opportunity, or it's nothing at all. It's all your choice.

Take your time on this. Do the work of looking and looking and looking patiently at this blank space till something that comes only from you and God working together begins to emerge. If it takes you a week or a year, so be it. It's your life! Take your time and see something.

For still the vision awaits its appointed time;
it hastens to the end—it will not lie. If it seems slow,
wait for it; it will surely come; it will not delay.

HABAKKUK 2:3 ESV

Have the Mind
of a Beginner

Have you ever heard the phrase, "Always have the mind of a beginner?"

How healthy would you become if they didn't tell you how healthy you could become? How many games would your team win if no one told them how many games they were supposed to win? You know, it could actually be really intelligent not to be very intelligent.

I was sitting with my father-in-law the other day, and he said to me, "Well, you know, there's not much life after you turn eighty." Actually, in the United States, that's true. I'm just amazed how people hit eighty, eighty-one, or eighty-two, and then that's about it.

That's not true in other countries. There are some people around the world still working into their hundreds. They are out in the rice paddies or in the shop or in the kitchen. Because they don't know they are supposed to be old and die at eighty. They just don't know any better.

It's interesting to me how we actually age (and fall apart) around our expectations and mind-sets. But what if you didn't know? What if you didn't know how fast your cancer was supposed to heal? Why not build your own timetable? That doesn't mean that you should go crazy and just do your own thing with wacky cures and other things. But what if you just didn't know? What if you just went out and lived your life? Good luck today.

—The Sender

Many, many good people are uncomfortable with the idea of a big, powerful life without borders or limits. It can be scary. It's like something within us needs boundaries and expectations in order to feel safety and comfort. We resist thinking bigger, and we even go as far as making excuses for ourselves about why we can't do this or that. Our lives morph into what we think we can or can't do and we become hardened into limits about ourselves that we believe are true.

And yet they aren't true. What you think is your limit is not real, and it's not God's idea for your life. God's idea for you is way bigger and involves stretching you to your limits.

Remember back when you were a kid, when you thought anything was possible? You thought that you could be an astronaut or a famous chef or maybe a rock star. You never stopped to think that you couldn't. "Can't" never even crossed your mind.

Then someone or something put a lid on it. They told you this or that about why you couldn't do whatever crazy thing it was that you wanted to do. Their opinion set as quickly as concrete, and it has never changed much inside of you. It has happened to all of us, and we live with those concrete barriers somewhere within our heads.

The remedy is to get back to being a beginner. Take yourself back to that place where anything is possible again. The child, the beginner, is not far away in your mind. On the lines that follow, take yourself to that place where you and God, the dynamic duo, are welded together into a composite new being that can do whatever you see yourself doing.

And let your presence and partnership in that place begin drawing new pictures in your mind of what your life could look like. Forget your age, and forget what you've learned to believe about yourself. And just go out and live it.

Jesus said, "Let the little children come to me,
and do not hinder them, for the kingdom
of heaven belongs to such as these."
Matthew 19:14

23

Happy Is a Byproduct

Charlie . . . I want you to think about byproducts. If you really want to be happy—a phrase that stands for so many things today; if you really want to have joy; and if you really want to be fulfilled, learn how to serve. Learn how to take your gift, give it to others, and learn how to serve.

We get so wrapped up in chasing the final product that we completely take our eyes off the process that gets us there. We chase our tails and we never get the prize.

You use your gifts, you serve people, you get absorbed in life, and happy comes. Happy is a byproduct.

Think of it like a coach: You do all the processes that win the game, and then the game wins itself.

So, I'll say it again: What do you want? Let's burrow down into the process and understand it well. I want to connect with my wife. I want to feel good about my marriage. I want a healthy body. These are all byproducts. They're all byproducts, Charlie.

What's the process that leads to the byproducts? Keep in front of you what you really want. And serve.

—The Sender

Find the word *happiness* in the Bible.

Alright, try *happy*.

Bzzzzzz. Not many entries, are there?

Look, we're not going to try to explain why something so esteemed in today's culture should make such a measly appearance in the Scriptures. But there's a useful lesson here.

The lesson is not that happiness isn't important, but that it appears after something else happens. It's a byproduct. In other words, you get to happiness by doing something other than grabbing for it directly. And the Bible is very, very clear about what that something is.

You really don't have to look any further than the Beatitudes (see Matthew 5:3–11) to find the answer. Jesus was teaching on a hill and He began to expound on the simplicity of living a good and productive life. Do you want to be happy? *Really* happy? Then read this Scripture over and over again, slowly and carefully. Understand that you're probably going to have to change your thinking and your lifestyle to put it into play.

If we believe what Jesus is saying here, we find that a deep and meaningful life is the byproduct of serving others. Put another way, happiness is the direct byproduct of selflessness. Swallow hard and listen, for this message is as popular today as it probably was back then. If you want to be happy, deeply joyous and peaceful, serve someone else. And be specific about it. Write down what you're going to do. Go out of your way to respect, help, and show kindness and love to someone specific in your life. Write their name down below. And don't expect anything in return. That expectation often chases away genuine peace. Rather, show up in the lives of specific people in your life without expectation, and happiness will chase you down. Happiness is a game that will win itself.

_Now when Jesus saw the crowds, he went up on
a mountainside and sat down. His disciples came to him,
and he began to teach them. He said: "Blessed are the poor
in spirit, for theirs is the kingdom of heaven."_

MATTHEW 5:1–3

24

"I'm Not Where I Want to Be, But..."

I work with my daughter's gymnastic team and her high school basketball team and I taught them this Gloria Gaither line today: "I'm not where I want to be, but thank God I'm not where I used to be."

People used to come in and see me for counseling. Most often I heard men and women complaining about each other. One day this woman came in all full of complaints that she couldn't find the perfect man. I suggested that we write out a list of the characteristics of the perfect man since she didn't have him at the time. So, she wrote down a list on my whiteboard: he's always good to me, good-looking, pleasant, loves kids, always in a good mood, and so on. Then I said, "Okay, would this kind of guy date you?" She got very mad at me. So, I suggested that we draw up a list of the characteristics of the kind of woman who would be the best match for that "perfect" man. Then I suggested that she focus on becoming the kind of woman who was on that list. I told her that it's not that that man hasn't shown up, but that she hadn't shown up herself . . . yet.

As two healthy men, let's you and me just keep each other accountable. Getting healthy. Becoming better men. Better fathers. And we are going to stay focused on our own lists. And we are going to teach that to your team: "I'm not where I want to be, but thank God I'm not where I used to be!"

—The Sender

Your next level in life is waiting for you. And when you arrive there, you will say, "Thank God I'm not where I used to be." The key to the journey might very well lie in this illustration of the woman looking for the perfect man.

Let's try this for your life: Make two lists for yourself. On the one list, write down what you want in your life. Three to five things. Be careful and honest about this, and write down what you deeply want. Then, on the other list, write three to five qualities you'll need to adopt to get those things on the first list. Our guess is that you spend more time thinking about what's on the first list than what's on the second list. That's pretty normal.

If you want what is on the first list, the qualities from the second list need to show up first. You will need to improve your game, advance a new vision, and stay focused on the new person who has yet to emerge. "I'm not where I want to be, but thank God I'm not where I used to be."

In Colossians 3:2, Paul talks of "setting your mind," as he says. Have you ever given any thought to what that means? It means being clear about focusing on higher things. It involves focusing not on what you want, but on who you want to become—who you need to become in order to take your life to the next level. That's what the Sender is talking about here.

When the second list person shows up, the game changes radically. Life becomes not a chase for what you want, but a clearly resolved picture of who you will be next. When the next-level person shows up, the "wants" will take care of themselves. And you might just be surprised at who you see.

For we walk by faith, not by sight.
2 CORINTHIANS 5:7 ESV

25

There Is a Plan for You

Hi, Charlie. These letters are your workout. These letters make your attitude strong. There are different muscles in our body. Attitude is one of those muscles. It's not a physical one, but a psychological one and a spiritual one. You know, Charlie, there is some research showing that divorce is higher among Christians than non-Christians. But interestingly, it seems it is not that way among Christians who go to church on some kind of regular basis. They are exercising their attitude toward marriage. This is my point: If you don't exercise a muscle, the muscle will atrophy and disaster follows.

So, here's the biggest workout of them all, believe this: There's a plan for you. Just a reminder, Charlie, there's a plan for you.

A man just called me from Florida and said his thirty-one-year-old wife has cancer. He sent me a picture of her walking on the beach with their two babies. He was crying on the phone. He goes, "Can you help me?"

The only reason he thinks I can help is because of what you and I have learned together. You know what I'm going to tell this wonderful young woman? There's a plan for her. Guess what else I'm going to tell her: Live in the vision, not in the circumstances. I'm going to tell her, "Listen, ma'am. It is not your condition; it's your position." Same stuff we've learned. Same stuff we've worked out on. Exercise, my man. Work it.

—The Sender

What you've been taught through your life may not be as important as what you've learned and worked out for yourself. What you learn and work out turns to muscle. And muscle turns to rock. Build your house on a rock.

In James 1:23–25, Jesus's brother James gives us a metaphor for this process of turning lessons into rock-hard muscle. Read it carefully and understand that the real work in learning lessons that last is practicing those lessons and working at them in a conscious, deliberate, on-purpose, moment-by-moment basis. Don't wander away from this mirror and forget the lesson. Instead, take your lessons and exercise them and turn them into your own personal muscle.

You can literally start that right now. Remember that many of us are passive learners. Lessons and ideas pass in and out of our heads without much thought or action. They drift in and out without any actual effort on our part. When you change this, when you to decide to activate those lessons as you learn them, another part of your brain becomes engaged and a deeper and more abiding permanence results. Have you experienced that?

Take your lessons deeper. Here's how to activate a lesson: Take a lesson you've learned in the last week and write it on the following lines. Then, next to that lesson, write something you can do today to take that lesson from passive to active. Be creative: How can you put action to that lesson in a way that serves others?

You want to know the best part? You can measure how effective you are at this. When you begin activating these lessons, you build your house on a rock that gets noticed. And the people you are meant to serve will be highly attracted to you. Be sure to make note of those who have been touched by the lessons you've learned and by the muscle you've built through your daily efforts.

*Anyone who listens to the word but does not do
what it says is like someone who looks at his face in a mirror
and, after looking at himself, goes away and immediately
forgets what he looks like. But whoever looks intently into
the perfect law that gives freedom, and continues in it—
not forgetting what they have heard, but doing it—
they will be blessed in what they do.*

JAMES 1:23–25

Leadership

Charlie, isn't it funny who leads? I heard this story in a TED Talks that I think may not be entirely accurate, but I still love it.

They put four monkeys in a room. They suspended a banana with a ladder, and all these monkeys started to scream and get all fired up. And when one monkey started up the ladder to get the banana, they sprayed all four with water. Then they brought in a new monkey and pulled one out. And they put the bananas up there again, and when the one new monkey went for the bananas, the other three pulled it down. Then they replaced another monkey. Same thing happened. Until they finally had four new monkeys in the room. None of them had been splashed with the water, but anytime one of them started up for the bananas the other three yanked him down, even though none of them had ever experienced the spraying water.

That's just about what happens today. We pull each other down, and we don't even know why. We just pull each other down. Until a leader steps up and changes things.

Keep leading, Charlie. Just keep on showing someone, "Here's the condition, but here's my position. Here's the circumstance. Here's my vision. Keep reaching up. There's no more water to be sprayed on you. That was a while ago. Don't be confused. Let me make sense of this. Follow me." That's leadership, Charlie.

—The Sender

There is a leadership dilemma we all need to address. We, each of us, live in the presence of phantoms that affect our ability to live purpose-driven lives. These phantoms are repeating ideas and thoughts and habits that don't appear to have any conscious origin. They've just taken root in our habits and run pretty much automatically. Things like *"I always deserve to be first in line"* or *"I'm too fat"* or quickly and thoughtlessly jumping to judge someone else. We probably didn't decide to think these things, yet they pop up in our minds over and over. And we follow them as if they are what we are actually choosing to be or do.

These thoughts and ideas flash by so fast we don't even take the time to examine or challenge them. They run on without control like a bunch of wild monkeys in a zoo.

Don't feel too bad; you're in good company. Paul complained of the same problem in Romans 7:15–19. It's a very human dilemma.

To us, a very simple definition of *leadership* is taking control of these phantoms and converting them into the thoughts we truly and thoughtfully want. Leadership in your mind is about controlling yourself and your own mind first, then letting others follow your brave and considered way of being.

Keep in mind an unbelievable advantage that you enjoy today. In Jesus's time, the illiteracy rate was generally regarded to be about 98 percent. Nobody could read or write. So, writing things, studying, planning, and applying deeply considered lessons to yourself was much tougher than than it is today. You have the chance, right now, to leap far ahead of your ancient predecessors and deeply write and think about who you are and where your life is going next.

Want to be more kind in all circumstances? Write it down below and focus on it. Do you want to look for opportunities to serve? Write that down below. Do you want to be more verbally brave in sharing with others how your mistakes and errors in life have shaped you? Write that down below.

Write and learn and take action. That's leadership and living with vision and purpose. That's living out the hard-earned lessons you deserve to enjoy.

Read the whole chapter of Romans 7 and know you are not alone in handling the monkeys in your own mind.

_____

_____

_____

_____

_____

_____

_____

_____

_____

_____

_____

*I do not understand what I do. For what I want to do I do
not do, but what I hate I do. And if I do what I do not want
to do, I agree that the law is good. As it is, it is no longer
I myself who do it, but it is sin living in me. For I know that
good itself does not dwell in me, that is, in my sinful nature.
For I have the desire to do what is good, but I cannot
carry it out. For I do not do the good I want to do,
but the evil I do not want to do—this I keep on doing.*

ROMANS 7:15–19

The Saucer Principle

Charlie, okay, here we go: Know your gifts, and how you've been blessed. Read Malachi 3:10: "See if I will not throw open the floodgates of heaven and pour out so much blessing that there will not be room enough to store it." In other words, I want to talk to you today about the gift that keeps on giving, especially as you are fighting what you are fighting. I'm going to teach you something called the Saucer Principle.

I kind of get blown away sometimes. I'm walking around in my beautiful home that my kids get to live in. The only blessing God gave me—and I'm not putting myself down—was yapping. Just talking. I walk around my house and I go, "This all came from talking. My kids live this way. I've been across the world. It's walked me into Israel. It's walked me into

Europe. I've spoken in every state. I actually met my wife through this. From just yapping."

David had many blessings, but one stood out: He could throw a rock. And when God gave him that blessing, he developed it by throwing at bears and lions who were attacking his sheep. Because he developed it, windows of opportunity opened, and he became the king of a nation. And these blessings overflowed to others for generations.

They were saucers, catching the overflow.

I want to show you where I'm leading you. The people around you, they are the saucers for you. From what you've learned and what you've done, your blessing is overflowing. And your players come to you with shaved heads. And they are the saucers. You have taken this blessing of coaching and your inspiration, and you have applied it to your illness and what you've learned is spillover to be caught in the saucers of all the others. Keep working your blessing. Even through your illness. Watch the saucers collect up all the blessing. It's the gift that keeps giving.

—The Sender

Being the first book in the Bible, a lot of focus is rightfully placed on the book of Genesis. But very little is said about

Malachi, the very last book of the Old Testament. Malachi is widely considered the final Old Testament prophet before the arrival of John the Baptist in the New Testament. His words should be taken seriously.

The Jewish people had gone through a lot and had relatively recently been released from Persian slavery to reestablish their Jewish homeland under Nehemiah. But life was tough: Harvests were poor and subject to constant locust damage, the Persians still held them under great political pressure. They had all but lost hope of their covenant promises and had become pretty indifferent and almost resentful toward God.

Malachi was calling them back, and reminding them of the promise of God to overflow their lives with blessings. Read Malachi 3:10.

We should expect no less in our lives today as that promise stands. The blessings are present, right now, in your life. Take a moment and count them. And the overflow? Let the overflow keep coming and expect it to fill the saucers that surround you.

You are surrounded by a complicated setting of saucers. Give this some thought. There are far more saucers around you than you might imagine. These include family, friends, friends of friends, online communities you are a part of, your children if you have them, and so on. The list might even include people you don't know yet. You are a patriarch/ matriarch in the making, and part of your job right now is appreciating your blessings, understanding how they over- flow, and becoming conscious of who your saucers are— then praying for them and serving them.

Your blessings will change the course of your life and the lives of many of those around you. Get to know your own saucers. Write their names down. Pray for them and care for them to the best of your ability. The opportunity to do this is the biggest part of your blessing.

And all these blessings shall come upon you and overtake you,
if you obey the voice of the LORD your God.

DEUTERONOMY 28:2 ESV

What's Your One Sentence?

Charlie . . . Claire Booth Luce was one of the first female congresswomen. She was worried that John F. Kennedy's message was becoming too splintered. So, she went up to him and said, "Mr. President, all great men are one sentence. Abraham Lincoln, he preserved the Union, he freed slaves. FDR, he lifted us out of the Great Depression and helped us win a world war. What's your sentence? It's clear to me but I want you to get clear on it."

Charlie, all great men are one sentence. The great ones are known by their one sentence. Give me one sentence that sums up you. There is great motivation with one sentence.

One of my favorite Scriptures is Acts 10:38. It sums this up so succinctly: "God anointed Jesus of Nazareth with the Holy Spirit and power, and . . .

he went around doing good." It doesn't get any better. Anointed by the Holy Spirit and all He does is go about doing good.

What's the one sentence? What's your sentence? Can I offer one to you? "Look at Charlie Christo, who found meaning in his cancer and became a better father, husband, friend, and coach as he goes about encouraging young men and inspiring others." How about that one? A better man.

But it can't be just clear to me. It has to be clear to you. So write it, my man!

—The Sender

Do the one-sentence exercise in the space following this devotion. But take it a step further: Write five sentences that define you. Just five short phrases that define you as wish to be. Take your time. These sentences may not come quickly, but that isn't the point.

Jaromir Jagr was the all-star hockey player for the Pittsburgh Penguins. He wore the number "68" on his jersey. When asked the significance of his number selection, he said that it stood for the year 1968, when his home country of Czechoslovakia was overrun by the Russians. His family suffered many casualties, and he wore the number to remind himself where he came from and that he was a fighter.

What's your "68"?

If you're searching a bit, consider Jesus's "68." Consider Acts 10:38, as referred to in the letter above. It's simple and potent. It says all that needs to be said. The phrase takes up little space, but it can fill an entire world with something special. Less really is more.

And if we could offer one more bit of wisdom on this: Don't think at all of how it will sound or look to others. What your one sentence is to others is what they see you do, not what you think you mean. Get it? This exercise is about perfect clarity within yourself. (You might notice that Jesus almost never talked about Himself. His task, His sentence if you will, revolved around being the light and shining, not talking Himself in circles about it. See how that works?) It's about personal clarity that turns to deliberate inner purpose that turns to action.

There would appear to be great power in bringing your one sentence into existence by writing it, then living it. What's your sentence?

_____

So, whether you eat or drink, or whatever you do,
do all to the glory of God.

1 CORINTHIANS 10:31 ESV

Wait with Expectation

Playoff time. Alright, Charlie. King David said, "I pray, O LORD, and wait with expectation." I wait with expectation.

Have you ever heard that Japanese children are much brighter than American children in mathematics? Recent research has found that's not true. At least one study has found that if you give an American child a mathematics problem that cannot be solved, the American child, a first-grader, quits on average at 9.47 minutes.

The Japanese child quits on average at 13.93 minutes. They are not smarter. They try harder. They keep going. When the reward isn't there, they keep going. When the cancer isn't cleared, do you keep going? When you haven't won the ball game, do you keep going, or do you pout and quit? Let's get honest. Most of us pout.

I read some of the work by the great Holocaust survivor Viktor Frankl. He said that in the Nazi concentration camps, the economy was cigarettes. And some people would be convinced that the war would end on such and such a date, and when that date hit and the war wasn't over, they sat down and smoked all their cigarettes and got very sick. They failed to wait with expectation.

In the book Good to Great, *Jim Collins talked about people who were lost at sea. He said they would be rescued at such and such a time. When they weren't rescued at that time, they gave up the will to live.*

Here's how to wait with expectation: "I don't know when I'm going to win this game, but I'm going to keep trying and not look at the scoreboard and not judge, but I am going to win this game."

Or try this: "I don't know when I'm going to be cured from cancer, but I am going to keep going and keep going. I have no timetable and when I'm cured, I'm cured."

Keep on doing what you are doing until you get what you want. And don't pout. Wait.

—The Sender

Admiral James Stockdale was the highest-ranking US naval officer held captive in the infamous "Hanoi Hilton" during the Vietnam War. He was shot down in 1965 and was not released for seven grueling years.

He was a leader among the prisoners and organized a communication system between the cells. He encouraged his fellow prisoners to resist the interrogation and torture by their captors. He became quite familiar with the mindset of all his men and what made them stronger as well as what weakened them.

He noted that prisoners who said, "We'll be released on this date," would crumble when that day came and nothing happened. The ones who survived and lived to see the day they were set free had a different mind-set. They said to themselves, in essence, "I don't know when I'm going to be free, but I'm going to be free." No firm date; no heartbreaking disappointment. Just learning to be strong in the wait.

The Bible is loaded with advice like this about waiting. (Go to openbible.info and search "*waiting with expectation*" for examples.) The message in all the verses is the same: Wait with expectation.

It does not say to be anxious and bite your nails. It says to simply wait. It does not say to set a date. It says to wait. It does not say to make deals with yourself and hustle and press. It says to wait. It does not say to become angry and pushy and mad. It says to wait. It does not say to lose hope and cry. It says to wait.

Waiting is something we all need to learn to practice better, particularly in times when answers and relief are far from clear or nearby. The results of God's greater good are things we must wait for; in God's time frame and not ours. So, waiting with patience and expectation is something we must master.

Write what you are waiting for and how you can wait with expectation.

_____

_____

_____

_____

_____

_____

_____

_____

_____

_____

_In the morning, LORD, you hear my voice;
in the morning I lay my requests before you
and wait expectantly._

PSALM 5:3

Wandering Generalities

Hi, Charlie. Have you read 1 Kings 18:21? Elijah was mad at the people because they were stuck between two competing beliefs. Most people are what I call "wandering generalities"—stuck between two competing opinions in their own minds. They've got all kinds of conflicting opinions in their heads. Sometimes even challenging each other.

Most often the simplest, clearest minds are the ones who choose to simply, peacefully have faith without competition or conflict.

Charlie, write out your prayers. That's what I've done. I write out my prayers. And then I can see what I pray. I see it in my head. See yourself as a healthy man. Keep seeing yourself as a healthy man who serves others. See your team as a championship team and you leading them and then taking that championship for a much higher purpose, like making those young men real men who serve others. Pray for God to release His angels to accomplish it.

Keep it very simple. Lock in on the picture. Not two different opinions, but victory in your health, victory in your family, victory on the field, and taking that victory and serving a much higher principle.

Faith is a choice. It's not a choice made on evidence. It's just a choice. Sometimes it's an outlandish, radical choice. But it still has to be a choice.

—The Sender

Following Christ, like being married, does not end with "I do." It is, in fact, the first of many steps that lead you in a new direction. It's a transformation that takes work and single-minded focus to be anything more than a difficult trudge.

Go to your Bible and read the 1 Kings 18 verse referred to in this letter. (In fact, read the entire passage, verses 16–39). Elijah was really hot about the people's unwillingness to clear their minds of conflicting thoughts and take action on God's plan. His demonstration was a great way to kill conflicting thoughts, though we don't recommend you trying this at home.

Clearing your mind of confusion and difficulty can be greatly aided by writing. And writing out your prayers and then praying them? Well, that's a good "conflicting thought killer" too—one that is very well worth trying.

So, write down your prayers. Then do as was suggested in the letter earlier: Read the prayer out and actively visualize the scenes, the words, the ideas. Take an orderly approach to this and do it well. Make scenes, words, and ideas clear in your mind, and the truth of them will follow.

If there is anything we've learned over our years, it's that personal empowerment and taking meaningful action in your life can be a fickle occurrence. It just doesn't show up as if by magic. No, it is a choice. And sometimes choices need to be buttressed and reinforced with live, vivid, faith-based cognitive decisions. Read that again: "live, vivid, faith-based cognitive decisions."

They create faith without being stuck on the horns of dilemma. Faith-based decisions create action without being caught in the crossfire of a mind that can't make itself up. Faith like this is born of a choice to do it and to remain consciously focused on what you have already decided. That kind of decision is empowering and uplifting to yourself and to others. Put the choice in front of you, make it, and don't think of it again. Move on in faith.

_____

_____

_____

_____

_____

_____

_____

_____

_____

_____

_____

_____

_____

Elijah went before the people and said,
"How long will you waver between two opinions?
If the LORD is God, follow him;
but if Baal is God, follow him."

1 KINGS 18:21

Failure of Imagination

Hi, Charlie. To do the impossible, you have to see the invisible.

C. S. Lewis, the writer of some of the best books on faith ever written, started off as an atheist. His best friend, J. R. R. Tolkien, was a Christian, and they had discussions, debates on spirituality, constantly. And in the very last one they had, J. R. R. Tolkien said something to C. S. Lewis that changed him. He said, "I'll tell you why you are an atheist. It's a failure of your imagination. You are not able to see it. Because you can't see it, you can't achieve it."

C. S. Lewis agreed with him, and he started to see. He started to understand. He started using his imagination, and few have moved others to faith in this modern era like the writer C. S. Lewis.

A child can dream. A child can create. A child can have a roaming, roaring, wild imagination. Then they quit using it, usually because an adult has scolded them into submission. They are taught more to memorize and repeat back facts. And their imagination dies. The priceless gift goes away.

Hey, Charlie, do you have any daydreams? Do you ever walk around in a dreaming state wondering, What if? Well, here's something to tell your team. Bobby Kennedy quoted George Bernard Shaw in a famous speech: "Some people see things as they are and say why? I dream things that never were and say, why not?"

There's always going to be doubt, Charlie. There's a book called The Cloud of Unknowing *written by a fourteenth-century monk about Christ in Gethsemane. It was about Christ's moment of doubt, His moment of wondering. We all have it. But in the end, asking yourself, "Why not me? Why not now?" transforms it all. Let your imagination grip that.*

—*The Sender*

This is a fascinating letter, and there is a lot going on here that is worth thinking about. Reread it carefully and write down any thoughts it might stir up. In so many ways, the ideas represented here are the fulcrum around which a powerful life is built: imagination, dreaming of things that aren't yet real but could be, asking yourself "why not?", surrendering to the unknown, and allowing yourself to think that maybe, with God's help, you could be a difference maker.

For the sake of this journal, take just one possibility and focus on it. The realm of possibility, the "upper-end dreamy possibility" for anyone is a total unknown. In truth, nobody knows how far or high or deep you are capable of going. About all we know is that we can do more. We can believe more. We can trust more. We can serve more . . . you get the idea.

Grasp on to the idea that the "more" we are referring to is about getting to know the real mind of God better. Not what He's doing, His activities, or His opinions, but getting to the unknown aspects of Him. If we let go of our need to see the actions of God and stop fighting the mysteries, His true nature begins to emerge. And you will know you are on the right track if you are totally surprised and awed by what you find. Because God is a complete and refreshing surprise. Think about that: He's well worth the effort to let go of your preconceptions and let His mysteries fill you with wonder and hope.

It's all there. Just let go and let Him.

---

*I have set the LORD always before me; because he is at my
right hand, I shall not be shaken.
Therefore my heart is glad, and my whole being rejoices; my
flesh also dwells secure. For you will not abandon my soul
to Sheol, or let your holy one see corruption.
You make known to me the path of life; in your presence
there is fullness of joy; at your right hand
are pleasures forevermore.*

PSALM 16:8–11 ESV

About the Authors

Bill Beausay is a full-time author and professional speaker. He has written nearly a dozen books, including three national bestsellers on parenting, leadership, and communication, and is a popular speaker on business topics related to activating high-potential professionals. His A-list of clients includes Exxon-Mobil, GE, Transamerica, Cisco, M.D. Anderson, University of Michigan, MDRT/2016, and dozens of Fortune 500 companies. Find out more about Bill at www.billbeausay.com,

Kevin Elko is a performance consultant, motivational speaker, and author of four books. He received his bachelor's degree in biology education and coaching, then went on to West Virginia University where he ultimately received his doctorate and was later inducted into West Virginia University Hall of Fame.

Elko's corporate clients have included ING, Tyson Foods, Abbott Labs, LPL Financial, The Hartford, Genworth, Jackson National Life, Pioneer Investments,

Morgan Stanley, Bank of America, Merrill Lynch, and Sun Life. He has worked with the Green Bay Packers and spoke to them the night before they defeated the Pittsburgh Steelers in the Super Bowl, the University of Alabama the night before they defeated LSU for the national championship, Alabama before they defeated Notre Dame for the national championship, and Florida State the night before they defeated Auburn for the national championship. Find out more about Kevin at www.drelko.com.

IF YOU ENJOYED THIS BOOK, WILL YOU CONSIDER SHARING THE MESSAGE WITH OTHERS?

Mention the book in a blog post or through Facebook, Twitter, Pinterest, or upload a picture through Instagram.

Share this book to those in your small group, book club, workplace, and classes.

Head over to facebook.com/worthypublishing, "LIKE" the page, and post an inspiring comment.

Tweet "I recommend reading #TheSender by @billbeausay // @drkevinelko //@worthypub"

WORTHY®

PUBLISHING

Visit us at worthypublishing.com